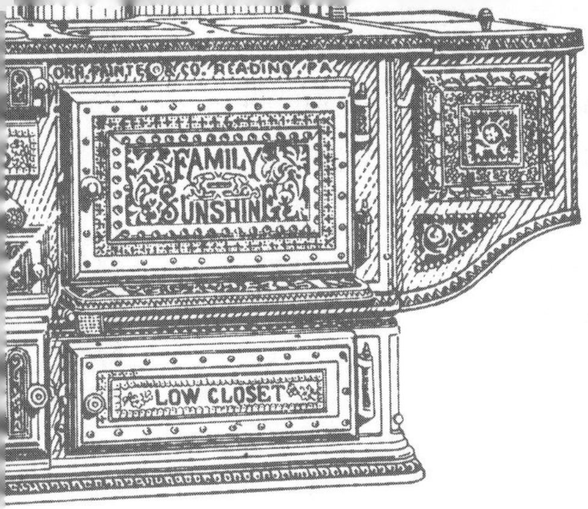

No. 15868.

height, 6½ inches; width, 4¼ inches; 4 inch dial; made by the celebrated New Haven Clock Company; lever movement, best grade nickel clock made, warranted. Price, 78c.

Beacon Luminous. No. 62911. Nickel Alarm Clock, with luminous dial; height, 6½ inches; width, 4¼ inches; 4 inch dial, and is manufactured by the New Haven Clock Company of New Haven, Conn.; best grade lever movement. Price, 97c.

NOTE — The dial on above clock is luminous, and will show distinctly the time in the dark. The darker it is the brighter it glows.

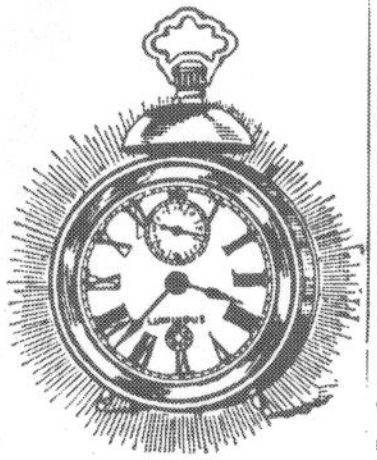

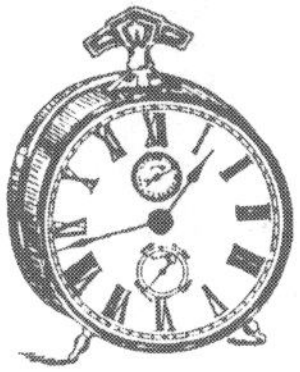

"Must Get Up." No. 62912. Nickel Alarm Clock; height, 5⅞ inches; dial, 4½ inches; made by the Waterbury Clock Company. This clock has very large bell on the back of the clock; the alarm runs five minutes with one winding; can be made to run a short, medium, long, or extra long time, and can be stopped at pleasure. The movement is best grade lever escapement and warranted. Price, $1.40.

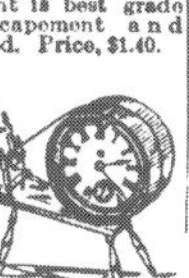

Spinning Wheel. No. 62913. Fancy Clock, in silver plate or gilt bronze finish; dial, 2 inches; beveled-edged glass; height, 8¾ inches; made by the Waterbury Clock Company; good lever movement; has no alarm. Price, $1.40.

Nos. 62914, 62915, 62915½.

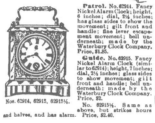

Patrol. No. 62914. Fancy Nickel Alarm Clock; height, 6 inches; dial, 2½ inches; has glass sides to show the movement; gilt front and handle; fine lever escapement movement; bell underneath; made by the Waterbury Clock Company. Price, $1.85.

Guide. No. 62915. Fancy Nickel Alarm Clock (similar to 62914); height, 7 inches; dial, 2½ inches; glass sides to show movement; gilt front and handle; bell underneath; made by the Waterbury Clock Company. Price, $2.

No. 62915½. Same as above, but strikes hours and halves, and has alarm. Price, $2.40.

Dorda. No. 62923. Polished, ebonized Wood Case, with gilt ornaments and gilt engraving; very fancy, in imitation of black onyx; height, 12 inches; length, 11 inches; dial, 4½ inches, with fine 8 day movement; made by the Waterbury Clock Company; strikes hours and half hours on cathedral gong bell. Your choice of

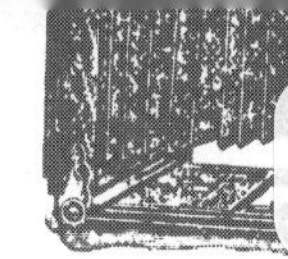

No. 6540.

No. 6540. The "Ideal" Camera is one of the best view cameras ever placed on the market. It is made of selected mahogany, is finished in the best possible style, every part being as nearly perfect as possible. All metal parts are made of brass, polished and lacquered.

The perfection of this camera is the result of much study and many experiments and is a favorite for both professional and amateur photography. It has reversible back with spring actuating ground glass frame, by which the plate holder is inserted between the ground glass and camera back. The bellows are cone shape but the 5 x 7 and all sizes above are made with fronts wide enough for stereoscopic lenses. By using a very simple method of attaching the horizontal swing it takes up no more room than does the single swing. The bed has two joints which admit of the use of lenses of short focus.

Sizes up to and including 6½ x 8½ are made the same as the above engraving; but sizes 8 x 10 to 11 x 14 inclusive are made similar to the "Empire State." The 14 x 17 and larger are made with back focus and with focusing handle instead of rack and pinion.

The price includes one perfection plate holder and canvas carrying case (which will hold three plate holders in addition to the camera) but has no lens or tripod. With sizes above 11 x 14 the English book plate-holder is furnished instead of the regular type of plate-holder.

Size of view.	Weight of camera.	Single swing.	Double swing.
3¼ x 4¼	2 lbs.	$14.45	$16.15
4 x 5	2½ "	15.30	17.00
4¼ x 6½	3 "	17.00	18.70
5 x 7	4½ "	18.70	20.40
5 x 8	4¾ "	20.40	22.10
6½ x 8½	5¾ "	22.10	25.80
8 x 10	8 "	25.50	28.05
10 x 12	9 "	28.05	30.50
11 x 14	12 "	32.30	35.70
14 x 17	23¾ "	42.50	46.75
17 x 20	30 "	51.50	57.80
18 x 22	38 "	61.20	68.00
20 x 24	46 "	76.50	85.00

THE CARLTON CAMERA.

Reversible Back.

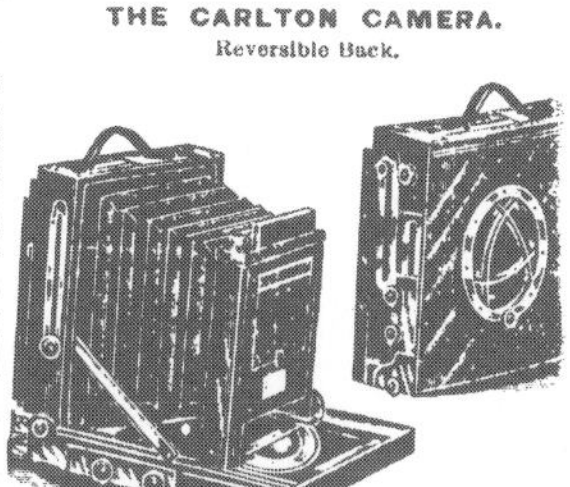

Partly Open. No. 6544. Closed.

No. 6544. The "Carlton" Camera without questi represents the highest perfection attained in profe sional view cameras. This camera has achieved gr popularity throughout the United States and Cana which it fully deserves as it is complete in every spect, with all modern improvements. Ideas

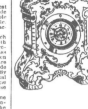

bury Company. Price, $1.65.

Boudoir No. 20.

) and 62

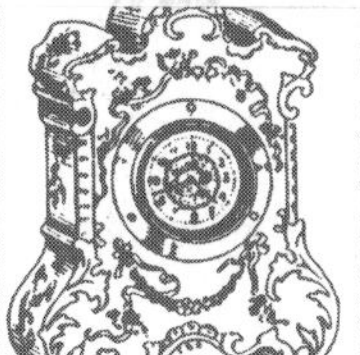

Boudoi No. 62922. Porcelain C mented wi colored, ha decorations 7½ inches; inches; bev 2 inch silve fine lever made by t bury Clock Price, $2.50.

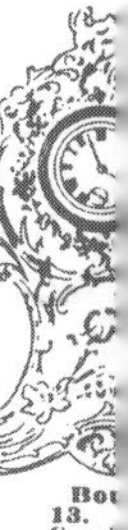

Ardmore. No. 62923. Fancy genuine imported Porcelain Case, with gilt and colored hand painted decorations; height, 9½ inches; width 5 inches; dial 2 inches, very fancy; made by the New Haven Clock Company. Price, $3.00.

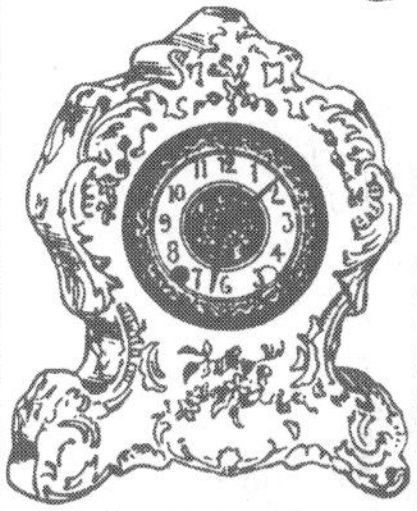

Nos. 62924 and 62925.

Bo 13. Genui lain C gilt a hand deco heig inches 7¼ in 3¼ in fine le men the Water Compa alarm $3.45.

Par 62925. import Porcel with colo painte tions; inches

7¼ inches; ivory dial, 3¼ inches; fancy gilt c gilt sash and bezel 8 day; strikes hours and on cup bell; has fine lever movement; made b brated Waterbury Clock Company. Price, $

RY STOVES.

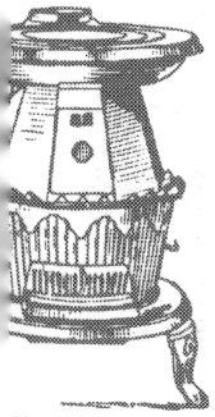

No. 15872.

ndry Sunshine, No. 11, a laundry stove, with brick er, with ring covers from d space on sides for nine lbs. Price, $5.40.

UNDRY STOVE.

or soft coal.

heap, convenient and ex- laundry stove, with two d door and dumping grate.

Weight.	Price.
67 lbs.	$2.82
80 lbs.	3.60
70 lbs.	3.00

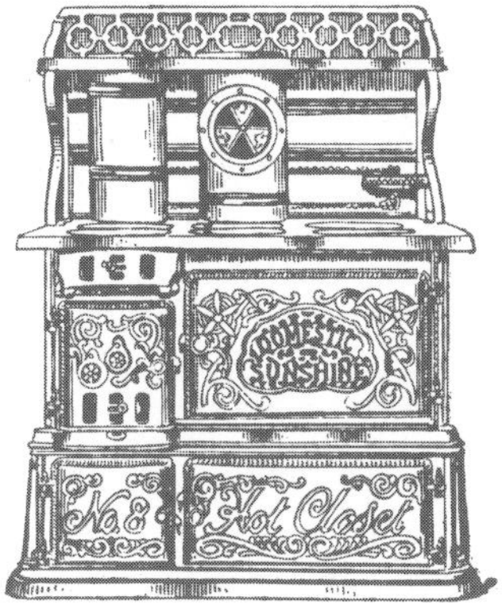

No. 15874.

DOMESTIC SUNSHINE RANGE.

For hard or soft coal.

No. 15874. This handsome range is the leading kitchener of its class. In its construction is embodied every practical improvement and convenience. An effective sifter prevents the possibility of any waste of fuel. The ash pan is so wide and capacious that no ashes can fall outside of it. Made only in one size. Has six covers.

Furnished with Duplex Grate.

No.	Size of covers.	Size of oven.	Size of fire box.	Size of hot closet.	Weight.
8	8 in.	13x19½x10½	7¾x8x14½	19¾x22½x8	456 lbs.

Price complete, with low closet and high shelf, $23.84.

R $22.50

R
ND

New Queen Sewing Machine

No. 91020

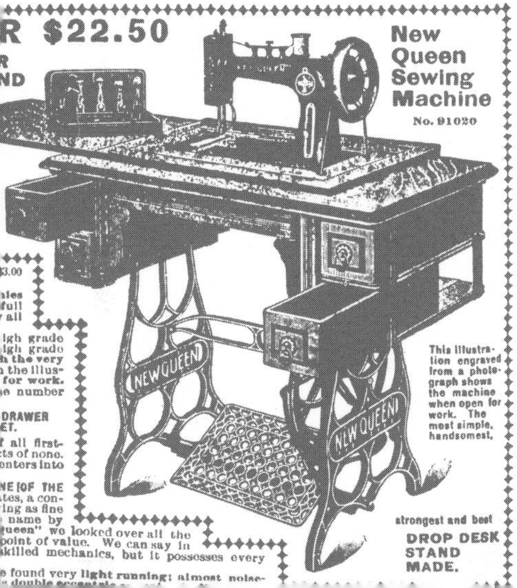

This illustration engraved from a photograph shows the machine when open for work. The most simple, handsomest, strongest and best

DROP DESK STAND MADE.

3.00

nies full all

igh grade igh grade the very the illus- for work. e number

DRAWER ET.

all first- ts of none. enters into

NE OF THE tes, a con- ing as fine name by ueen" we looked over all the point of value. We can say in skilled mechanics, but it possesses every

e found very light running; almost noise-

OUR SPECIAL OFFER: SEND US $5.00 as a guarantee of good faith and we will send you the suit by freight. C. O. D., subject to examina can examine it at your freight depot, and if found perfectly satisfactory pay the freight agent the balance, $18.00 a Three per cent. discount allowed if cash in full accompanies your order, when $22.31 pays for the suit.

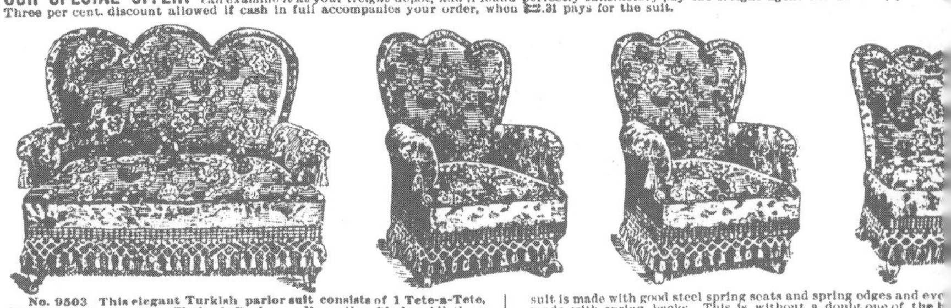

No. 9503 This elegant Turkish parlor suit consists of 1 Tete-a-Tete, 1 Rocker, 1 Gents' Easy Chair, 1 Parlor or Reception Chair. All these pieces are made in extra large size, high backs and large comfortable seats, and are very latest design. The upholstering or cover of this suit is in the latest design and pattern of imported goods; each piece is covered in a different color. We will be pleased to mail you samples of six different colors to select from, or if left to us to make selection in colors our upholsterer will in all cases give you colors on this suit that will please you in every respect. The suit is finely upholstered, with plush band and rolls on top and sides of back and trimmed with a heavy worsted fringe. This suit is made with good steel spring seats and spring edges and eve made with spring backs. This is without a doubt one of the b suits ever put on the market at the price we ask for it and will b ment in any home. We can furnish this same parlor suit upholste grade of crushed plush, assorted colors, and other styles of coveri

4 piece Parlor Suit, price in cotton tapestry..........
4 piece Parlor Suit, price in crushed plush..........
4 piece Parlor Suit, price in silk brocatelle..........
4 piece Parlor Suit, price in silk damask..........

A $35.00 PARLOR SUIT FOR $24.00.

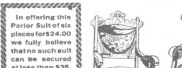

In offering this Parlor Suit of six pieces for $24.00 we fully believe that no such suit can be secured at less than $35,

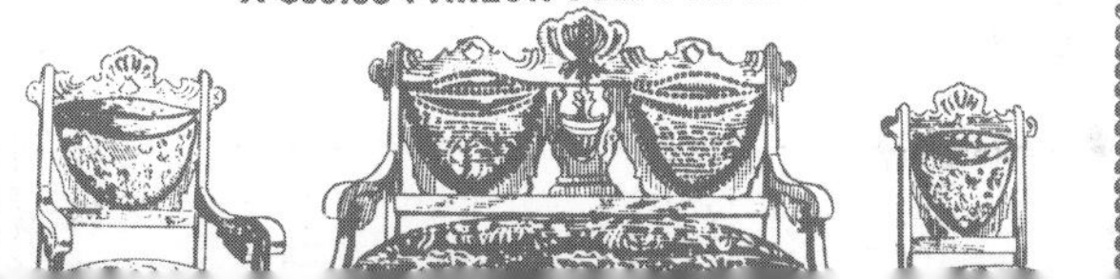

Made w solid oak solid birch If furnish solid birch finished in

Urban Life

LIFE IN AMERICA 100 YEARS AGO

Urban Life

Linda Leuzzi

Chelsea House Publishers

New York   Philadelphia

CHELSEA HOUSE PUBLISHERS
Editorial Director: Richard Rennert
Executive Managing Editor: Karyn Gullen Browne
Copy Chief: Robin James
Picture Editor: Adrian G. Allen
Creative Director: Robert Mitchell
Art Director: Joan Ferrigno
Manufacturing Director: Gerald Levine

LIFE IN AMERICA 100 YEARS AGO
Senior Editor: Jake Goldberg

Staff for *URBAN LIFE*
Assistant Editor: Annie McDonnell
Assistant Designer: Lydia Rivera
Picture Researcher: Sandy Jones
Cover Illustrator: Steve Cieslawski

First Printing

1 3 5 7 9 8 6 4 2

Library of Congress Cataloging-in-Publication Data

Leuzzi, Linda.
    Urban life/Linda Leuzzi.
        p. cm.—(Life in America 100 years ago)
    Includes bibliographical reference and index.
    ISBN 0-7910-2841-0
    1. United States—Social life and customs—1865–1918—Juvenile literature. 2. City and
town life—United States—History—19th century—Juvenile literature.I. Title. II. Series.
                                                                                    94-24617

E168.L65 1995   CIP

973'.09732—dc20   AC

CONTENTS

LIFE IN AMERICA 100 YEARS AGO

Health and Medicine

Law and Order

Manners and Customs

Rural Life

Transportation

Urban Life

Urban Life

The Growth of Cities

IF YOU WERE TO WALK DOWN 55TH STREET ON THE EAST Side of New York City around the turn of the century, you would find mostly brownstone homes. While each single-family house had its own distinctive look, with an ornate front gate or a handsome door with beveled glass, they all had stoops and usually four floors, plus a basement entrance for the deliveries. Even at this time, many of the large front windows were protected against burglars by fancy iron grilles. On Fifth Avenue near Central Park, Irish nurses pushed bundled infants in baby carriages down wide, tree-lined paths.

Downtown on Cherry Street, you would not find such glamorous surroundings. Dingy brick facades covered the tenement houses, which rose seven or eight stories high. They were mean-looking buildings with zigzagging iron fire escapes crowded with household items. A worn-looking mother on the street might be seen shoving a pail under gushing water from a fire hydrant. It was a little easier than waiting in line at the sinks with pumps in the hallway. Either way, the water still had to be hauled up several flights of stairs.

Pushcart peddlers on Hester Street on New York's Lower East Side. Although the city was a lure for new immigrants, many of them came from quiet country areas and the city was a shock to them. Gone were the seasonal work patterns of rural life and the generations of village families they shared their lives with. To ease the adjustment, many people of the same nationality chose to live together in ethnic neighborhoods. Hester Street was the place to live for newly arrived Jewish immigrants. Jostling among the pushcart vendors, they sought advice on lodging, jobs, and anything else they needed. Street vendors were a vital part of the economies of immigrant neighborhoods, selling cheese, chickens, fish, pretzels, vegetables, and dry goods.

Loud voices came through the open door from the hordes of families who lived there, and some ragged children ran out. Don't breathe deeply; the unpleasant smells are powerful.

New York wasn't the only city at this time with contrasting neighborhoods of great wealth and poverty; other major urban centers like San Francisco, Boston, Cincinnati, Chicago, and St. Louis

A view of Broadway, New York City, in 1880. Broadway's roots go back a long way. Initially used as a trail by Native Americans, it developed into a main road leading out from the fort of New Amsterdam into the colonial wilderness. It was first known as Beaver's Path, then renamed Heere Straat, or Gentlemen's Street. Finally, the Dutch named it Breede Wegh and the name stuck.

had both prosperous and miserable sections as well. Yet by 1900, 40 percent of the American population had chosen to live in cities, and between 1860 and 1915, 2,000 urban centers had developed. How did American cities begin, why did they grow, and what was the lure for both the rich and the poor?

Initially, when the country was young, if a ship could reach and depart from a location with relative ease it was a good place to settle. New Amsterdam, on Manhattan Island, had the best harbor on the continent, a protected place with deep waters where ships could

11

Philadelphia in 1874, as viewed from the South Street Bridge. The plan of most American towns in the 18th century was laid out on a grid—that is, in the form of rectangular blocks bounded by parallel streets that ran in two directions, crossing each other at right angles. Philadelphia was a grid city. Chosen by William Penn in 1682, its grid was planned on a site 100 miles up the Delaware River where it joined the Schuylkill River. It was one of the main colonial cities built along the Atlantic coast with a deep harbor, and was easily the largest city in the country by the time of the Revolution. It had one of the nation's first public water companies. Water was pumped through wooden pipes to a reservoir on high ground, enabling the city's residents to have running water.

Washington, D.C., in 1903. George Washington laid the Capitol Building's cornerstone in 1793. The Capitol's dome was still unfinished when Lincoln was elected and he made it his priority to complete the dome and add more government structures. Mark Twain's description of Washington as a "wide stretch of cheap little brick houses with here and there a noble architectural pile lifting itself out of the midst" was accurate, and it took more than a century for the nation's capital to achieve its architectural prominence. The Washington Monument was a good example of the slowness, disinterest, and lack of financing that plagued the city's growth. Begun in 1848, work stopped on the monument in 1854 and wasn't resumed until 1879 when Congress voted for funds to complete it. Architect Pierre Charles L'Enfant's plan called for a grand sweep of radial avenues around the monument, but the work was canceled and not resumed until 1900, after the appearance of the City Beautiful Movement at the World's Columbian Exposition in Chicago in 1894. This photograph shows the view from the Treasury Building down Pennsylvania Avenue, looking toward the Capitol.

anchor. It also had the Hudson River, a fine waterway for boats to navigate into the interior of the country. Boston, situated at the mouth of the Charles River, also featured a natural harbor. Newport, Rhode Island, had an excellent anchorage, as did Charleston, which jutted out between the Ashley and Cooper rivers in South Carolina. And while Philadelphia was 100 miles from the sea, the ocean could be

A street scene in one of New York's immigrant ghettos. At the turn of the century, 40 percent of the country's population lived in cities with populations of 2,500 or more. At this time, I percent of the nation's families controlled 88 percent of the nation's wealth. Inner-city residents were generally forced to live in small apartments with little or no sanitation facilities. While the rich had homes that took up whole blocks, the poor were jammed into cramped quarters. In New York, a single tenement could house nearly 150 people; a single block of these tenements might house 2,500 people. Boston had similar problems. In 1905, about one-third of its 80,000 residents were squeezed into single rooms in the city's South End.

reached via the Schuylkill and Delaware rivers. These seaport cities thrived commercially by serving as centers of trade, exporting agricultural products from western farmers and importing finished manufactures from Europe.

While there was no doubt that the coastal cities were the lifelines of economic vitality, it was also true that the country was mainly

Street kids. Because slum areas were jammed with buildings, yards and parks were virtually nonexistent and there were few green areas for children to play. Children had to play in the streets and dodge traffic. They congregated in poorly ventilated hallways or on rooftops. That was when they weren't working. In order to make ends meet, many parents and their children worked together inside their apartments in cottage industries making cigars, artificial flowers, or clothing. Their wages averaged two to four cents an hour.

rural in the early years. By 1790, only 24 cities had over 2,500 residents, accounting for only 5 percent of the entire population. The lure to push farther inland, to own land, and to farm was a stronger attraction than the cities for the many immigrants who crossed the Appalachian Mountain range and settled in the Ohio Valley. New cities sprouted up along the Ohio and Mississippi rivers, where agricultural goods were taken downstream by rafts or boats to gulf towns. Many western cities, far away from eastern markets, expanded out of necessity because transporting goods was so costly. They established a certain degree of self-sufficiency by building mills and factories that turned out everyday items normally brought from the East.

Of all the emerging technologies in the 19th century, transportation had the greatest effect on the growth of cities. Robert Fulton's steamboat, launched in 1807, made the trip up the Hudson River from New York City to Albany and back in five days. The steamboat was soon adapted to work in the shallower waters of the great Mississippi River and its chief tributary, the Missouri, which trailed

This beautiful structure was the New York mansion of Charles Schwab, which stretched from Riverside Drive to West End Avenue between 73rd and 74th streets. Schwab was head of United States Steel, the world's first billion-dollar corporation. His mansion, called Riverside, was a 75-room home constructed of cream-colored granite with 116-foot-high pinnacles, probably the most spectacular home built in New York at the time. Andrew Carnegie, who lived on Fifth Avenue in what is now the Cooper-Hewitt Museum and was himself one of the richest men in America, commented about the Schwab residence, "It makes mine look like a shack."

The main reception area of the William Randolph Hearst residence on Riverside Drive and 86th Street in New York. Hearst was an outrageous, unscrupulous, and eccentric newspaper publisher. When the top three floors of the 12-story Clarendon apartment house became too cramped for the tycoon and his accumulated antiques and artwork, Hearst bought the whole building and evicted the eighth and ninth floor tenants so that he could construct this baronial reception room with 35-foot-high ceilings.

west. Cities like St. Louis, located just below the point where the Mississippi merges with the Missouri, boomed in commercial business and passenger travel. On the South's Red River alone, at least 30 landings had developed along the 500-mile stretch of river above Shreveport, Louisiana, by the time of the Civil War.

Canals began to appear on the American landscape, linking inland areas to major cities. In 1825, the completed Erie Canal joined New York's capital of Albany to the state's most western city, Buffalo. Small cities, wanting to grow, campaigned for inclusion on the canal routes built between 1816 and 1840. The emergence of railroads spurred growth in many nearby towns. Atlanta, Georgia, and

Birmingham, Alabama, developed into major cities because of their location near the junction of two important rail lines.

Cities didn't begin experiencing much population growth until 1820, when European famines, revolutions, and wars drove a huge wave of immigrants to our shores. European governments, which had previously opposed the emigration of skilled workers, were now facing overpopulated cities and no longer discouraged those who wanted to leave. A majority of the newcomers were Irish and German with mostly country roots, but they arrived with little or no money and found it difficult or impossible to travel further to a rural area. Many stayed in the cities they arrived in, or traveled to secondary cities like Providence or Paterson, New Jersey. More than five million Europeans had landed in America by 1860, settling mainly in the Northeast.

Before there were stereos or radios, if people wanted to have music in their homes they had to make it themselves. It was not uncommon for a well-to-do middle-class family to own a piano, and instead of new record releases people clamored for the latest printed sheet music. Bands, orchestras, and choral societies performed frequently both indoors and outdoors, and all the music was live.

Almost a caricature of herself, a well-to-do woman walks her dog down the street. Throwing grand parties, shopping for the latest fashions, and supervising the household staff were the main activities of rich society women. But some were involved in philanthropic and charity work, and some were activists. Louisine Elder Havermeyer gave her vast collection of paintings to the Metropolitan Museum of Art when she died. Alva Belmont was an important figure in the women's suffrage movement.

Women were adding their numbers significantly to the cities' workforce, especially in factories. By 1831, women took the lead in employment in the textile industries. There were women shopkeepers in every city selling books, dry goods, and other items, as well as skilled women artisans who might be printers, tailors, and hatmakers. Forced out of their traditional role as midwives with the professionalization of nursing, women turned to teaching as their chief occupational mainstay.

While not as large as the arrival of the Europeans, Chinese migration through San Francisco began around the time of the California gold rush. Between 1848 and 1881, about 300,000 Chinese came to the United States, mostly from Canton in southern China.

Many of those who settled in the mountainous mining districts moved on to San Francisco, establishing the country's first Chinatown. They worked in mining, agriculture, manufacturing, and as domestics and laundry workers. Their labor was essential in completing the western route of the Central Pacific Railroad and creating a transcontinental railroad system.

Between 1860 and 1910, city populations increased sevenfold, mainly as a result of overseas immigration. But many of the children of western farmers also began to move to the cities. Modern farm equipment—harrows, reapers, and harvesters—made farming much more productive, freeing up surplus agricultural labor. With the mechanized, self-raking reaper, a farmer could cut down 12 acres of wheat in one day. That was a big leap in productivity for the farmer; with the traditional cradle scythe, only two acres could be cut down manually. Increased productivity also drove prices down, making farmers push to till more land to make up for the difference. Machinery was harvesting 80 percent of America's wheat by 1880. As markets became glutted with farm goods and prices fell, farm poverty increased. The work was also hard and lonely. Some people went west looking for new opportunities, but many farm workers sought city employment.

Spurred by the poverty, oppression, and violence they experienced in the rural South, black Americans began moving to northern and western cities by 1890, creating communities that would serve as magnets for the larger black migration that occurred during World War I. While factory jobs might be available to immigrants, they were not always open to blacks. Some gained professional positions, but for the most part they were employed within the service industries. By the end of the century, over 30 cities developed significant black populations of 10,000 or more. During the colonial period, about 600,000 Europeans and 300,000 Africans came to our shores. About half of the Europeans, mostly English, came here as indentured servants. By the time of the Revolution, Africans or their descendants constituted one-fifth of the population.

In the 19th century, mostly Scotch-Irish and Germans immigrated. Between 1820 and 1860, 90 percent of the immigrants who came were from the British Isles and northwestern Europe; they continued to dominate immigration again between 1882 and 1890. These English, Irish, German, and Scandinavian groups who landed in Boston and New York were similar to the original colonists in looks, customs, and religion, and they blended in with the mainstream.

After 1880, a different group began to arrive. This group came from southern and eastern Europe. They were called "new immigrants" because of their different looks and customs. Steamships provided a way out for the peasants who wanted a better life, and crossing the Atlantic was now possible in a matter of days instead of weeks. The cost of a ticket was low; passengers who sailed steerage class (named because it was near the steering equipment) on these liners paid about $20 for the voyage. While poor, most could afford passage for their families by selling everything they had; others were helped financially by family members who had already come to America and found work.

The weary newcomers were the targets of unscrupulous people who promised jobs, housing, and other basic services and then swindled them out of their money. "I have met with so much deception since we have landed on the shores of the New World that I am fearful of trusting anyone," wrote one immigrant. To both

Charles Square, Boston, in 1906. In the early 20th century, Boston tried to impose restrictions on the height of buildings in an effort to preserve its skyline. In 1909, Harvard University offered the first courses in urban planning.

protect and control the immigrants, the federal government established Ellis Island.

Ellis Island, an immigration station located on three acres of land in the upper New York harbor, opened in 1892. Unfortunately, in the early days the problems the immigrants experienced at the docks were repeated by Ellis Island employees who overcharged for food, cheated the immigrants in money exchanges, and blatantly hinted at bribes that would make the processing easier. Humaneness was minimal. Those who were detained there ate on dirty dishes in the dining room or did not eat at all. In an effort to eliminate corruption and reform the mistreatment of immigrants, Theodore Roosevelt initiated major changes after his election as president.

But even with the reforms, the process was bewildering. The immigrants trooped off the boats with bulging valises and bundles, sometimes standing on line for hours before entering the building. Then they began to worry. Would they pass the doctor's inspection? What if they answered questions the wrong way? And what was to be expected if they had to stay overnight?

"They had quite a few cots in a big room and a lot of people," wrote Bessie Spylios, an 11-year-old Greek girl, who described her overnight experience at Ellis Island in 1909. "You slept with your boots and the way you came was the way you went to bed. There was no place to get undressed. Just lie down and sleep. And get up in the morning ready to travel."

Austro-Hungarians, Italians, and Russians comprised the three largest "new immigrant" groups. In the old countries, they had been victims of heavy taxes, religious persecution, and land laws that made it impossible to farm. American cities became a major lure for the immigrants for several reasons. The steel, mining, and lumber industries were experiencing huge growth. America was in the midst of its Industrial Revolution and technological innovations occurred at a rapid pace. Alexander Graham Bell's telephone had been patented in 1876, and telephone factories were centered in Boston and Chicago. Thomas Alva Edison invented the light bulb in 1879, and his first public generating station was supplying power to customers in 1882. Henry Ford began to produce a gasoline car in 1896; between 1911 and 1912, his Detroit factory cranked out 78,000 Model T cars. The new immigrants needed jobs; the cities with these industries and their offshoots had them.

State Street, Chicago, in 1899. State Street became a major business center after it was rebuilt following the Great Chicago Fire in 1871. Note the cable car tracks. Cable cars were actually used much more widely in Chicago than in San Francisco.

Factories sprang up everywhere; the number of those with 10,000 or more workers almost doubled during the last two decades of the century. Cheap immigrant labor produced shoes in Cincinnati and Rochester, New York, textiles in Fall River, South Dakota, bikes in Chicopee, Massachusetts, and paper in Holyoke, Massachusetts. The immigrants clustered in the northern cities and on the Pacific Coast.

Most immigrants sought out the ethnic colonies already established in cities, where old country friends offered familiar conversation and advice on finding a place to stay. These colonies were usually in the poorer districts or in the city's outskirts. Not all of these areas were squalid, but by 1915, President Wilson's Industrial Commission reported, one-third, and perhaps as much as one-half, of manufacturing or mining wage earners did not earn enough in one year to support themselves in comfortable and decent conditions.

But even with these prevailing realities, the city's pull was strong. Back in the old countries, getting an education and attending cultural activities was virtually impossible. Here, education was free and libraries and museums were open to everyone at no charge. Kindergarten was available and vocational centers with evening instruction made it possible to learn new skills. There were lecture series spoken in native languages on local government and American history. These were opportunities the immigrants never dreamed they could take advantage of.

City Life: Growth and Upheaval

THE NEW IMMIGRANTS SWELLED THE POPULATIONS OF THE cities and brought about violent upheaval and growth. New technologies had a similar effect. A good example was the horsecar trolley line, which did more than just transport city residents. These lines impacted downtown areas significantly because of the teeming masses of people they brought back and forth daily, resulting in a surge of business activity. Brick and stone commercial blocks sprouted up and new factories appeared. In places like Boston, landlords who owned four-story buildings along these horsecar routes converted the ground floors for commercial use, while the remainder housed families. A mile or two away from these districts, detached houses were being constructed.

To accommodate commuters in the outer areas, horse trolleys required street extensions. Longer routes called for additional street lights along the way as well as more police and fire protection. The introduction of cable cars, bridges, and elevated railroads and subways also resulted in urban expansion. Eventually, by the 1880s,

Times Square, New York, in 1907. Times Square was originally known as Long Acre Square, a wide crossing at the intersection of Seventh Avenue and Broadway. Broadway was the only city street that did not follow the rectangular grid plan instituted in 1811. It cut diagonally across avenues and created open spaces. In the 1890s, blacksmiths did their business here, as did the carriage trade, fixing and repairing horse-drawn vehicles. In 1895, Oscar Hammerstein opened the Olympia Music Hall on the east side of Times Square between 44th and 45th streets. When the *New York Times* opened its new building at the south end of the Square in 1904, the area was renamed Times Square.

the unwieldy arrangement of telephone, electricity, and high-voltage trolley cables on poles and overhead wires had become dangerous, and New York was the first city to plan conduit tunnels. That meant major city streets had to be torn up. New schools, civic buildings, water mains, and sewers became urgent necessities as increasing populations flowed in.

Gone were the days when a city's residents all knew one another. Industrial development and the impact of the immigrants overwhelmed city governments. It was impossible for most city councils to fund urban improvements quickly and cheaply, and impatient residents appealed to state legislatures. As a result, state boards and commissions were established, and the self-governed American city began to disappear. In many cases, the infamous "boss" system emerged.

Businessmen familiar with pricing and what was necessary to get the job done were selected to oversee these boards and commissions. Some were in the construction business and often awarded contracts to their own firms or those of friends, who then gave kickbacks to commissioners. Other officials sold franchises to public utilities. Political "machines" evolved; their main functions were to gain power and to make money.

In some cities, these machines became particularly entrenched. New York's William "Boss" Tweed, who became the Grand Sachem of Tammany Hall in 1868, is probably the most famous example. Tammany Hall, which originally started as a club in 1789, was also the most powerful of the four Democratic committees in the city and had its own headquarters. Tweed was already an experienced and wily politician by the time he took the Grand Sachem post, and his skill with political rings snared votes for key bills. One of Tweed's gold-mine projects was the construction of a new county courthouse at $12,500,000, an outrageous amount at the time. An example of the padding: the cost of thermometers totaled $7,500; brooms were listed at $41,190; spitoons were $190 each; and plastering had cost the city $2 million. By 1871, at age 47, Tweed was supposedly worth $12 million. While he was generous with himself and others, New York City's debt rose from $300 million to $900 million during his tenure. He was eventually convicted of 104 counts of bribery and fraud and died in jail.

The political machine controlled people through bribes and corruption. It also offered protection. Transport and utility corporations paid to ward off competition. Gamblers and prostitutes paid to keep their illegal businesses going. The entrenchment of machines in the cities became strong, in many cases because of sentimental loyalties. Many of the bosses were first or

Electric trolleys in Denver, Colorado, in 1885. Denver was the biggest city of the Rocky Mountain region. A tough frontier settlement that served to supply local gold miners, its citizens raised $280,000 to build a rail line to their city from Cheyenne, Wyoming, when the Union Pacific Railroad bypassed Denver as a stop. With lots of money from the gold fields, Denver could afford to install the latest innovations in transportation.

Women office workers. By 1900, 20 percent of the nation's women were wage earners. Five percent of the nation's doctors were women, and some managed to succeed as lawyers, engineers, scientists, and corporate managers. Their careers also included teaching, social work, and managing the settlement houses. They also worked as machine laborers in the textile industries, and, as shown here, as clerks in offices. Unfortunately, there was no minimum wage law for women and some worked for salaries as low as $6 to $8 a week, well below the wages paid to men for the same jobs.

second-generation immigrants, and represented role models for the newcomers. They met with them as they struggled off the boats and arranged jobs and housing in exchange for their votes. The requests were easy to grant because most immigrants started out with so little. Encouraging words and the assurance of a few basic services went a long way in cementing political loyalties, especially when no city services offered these things. Most bosses were well known for their generosity to the poor; holiday dinners were paid for and sizable contributions were made to hospitals and libraries.

A national movement for reform evolved as scandals about political patronage were revealed in the newspapers. The National Law Enforcement League was formed in New York in 1883, and the group campaigned in several cities. Bureaus of municipal research,

A magazine cartoon of Cornelius Vanderbilt. Vanderbilt made his enormous fortune by merging several large railroad companies in the 1860s. This cartoon shows him standing in the middle of his empire, holding the strings. A sign says, "All freight seeking the sea board must pass here and pay any tolls we demand." Vanderbilt was ruthless, corrupt, and did not care about the public or the law. He paid one New York legislator $75,000 as a bribe to support his takeover of the Erie Railroad.

established in New York, Philadelphia, and Cincinnati between 1906 and 1908, served as watchdogs over the cost of materials and procedures. Muckraking, a term Theodore Roosevelt used unfavorably to describe writers exposing corruption, was popular among journalists from 1902 to 1912. Magazines ran in-depth

Andrew Carnegie. Carnegie was a 13-year-old Scottish immigrant when he came to this country. As a young man, he worked in a cotton mill and as a messenger in a Pittsburgh telegraph office, where he learned the art of telegraphy. A Pennsylvania Railroad official recognized his potential and gave him a job. Carnegie then worked his way up in the railroad industry. In 1873, he switched businesses and opened his own steelworks in Pittsburgh. The Carnegie Steel Company eventually grew into a large conglomeration of steel mills, railroads, mines, and other businesses, and by the turn of the century Carnegie had become one of the world's richest men. He lived quietly and modestly, and eventually sold his company to J. P. Morgan for nearly half a billion dollars. In 1901, he retired from industrial life and became a philanthropist, eventually giving away more than $350 million for various causes and the construction of public buildings. New York's famous Carnegie Hall is named after the industrialist, who funded its construction.

articles targeting the corrupt practices of giant companies and city administrations, naming names and detailing incidents. The passion and tenacity these journalists put into their articles had its impact; reforms were made in business and at least one piece of legislation, the Pure Food and Drug Act, was passed as a result of their work.

The housing boom continued. The square-grid formation was the basic pattern for most city streets. Americans liked openness, and early on, when many of these grids were yet to be developed, a

Like Carnegie, John D. Rockefeller was a self-made man. He became a partner in a Cleveland trading house when he was only 19. He made a fortune during the Civil War, and in 1870 he formed the Standard Oil Company of Ohio. Like many of the industrialists of the time, Rockefeller believed in free enterprise only so long as it worked for him, and he crushed his competition ruthlessly. He eventually owned a vast network of oil refineries in Cleveland, Pittsburgh, Philadelphia, Baltimore, and New York.

person could stand in almost any area of the city and look out over fields and woodlands. Some of these plots were used to plant gardens, to keep a cow or a goat, or as grassy playgrounds for children.

But that changed in the later part of the 19th century, as industry and populations increased. The Stuyvesant, built in 1869 in New York, was the first building of its kind—a multiple-dwelling structure for the upper-middle class. Ten years later, Edward Clark, who

Inventor Charles T. Harvey demonstrates his elevated railroad on an experimental half-mile track above Greenwich Street in lower Manhattan in 1868. Harvey dressed for the occasion in a top hat and formal coat. He climbed onto the track, settled into his car, and drove it at five miles per hour while spectators cheered. Harvey's car was pulled along the track by a cable attached to a stationary steam engine at one end of the line, but the cable kept breaking, so small steam engines were installed on each car, making them self-propelled. Elevated rail lines, or "els" as they were called, became a major form of urban transportation until the rail lines were put underground.

Some of the elevated lines and their stations were beautiful works of modern steel architecture, resembling little Alpine homes with pavilion roofs and wrought iron trim. The steam engines that first pulled the cars, however, generated too much noise and spewed out soot and cinders over the streets; they were eventually replaced with electric motors.

headed the Singer Sewing Machine Company, became one of the biggest developers of New York's Upper West Side. Clark began with 27 elegant single-family townhouses on 73rd Street, west of Central Park. But his sterling achievement was the Dakota, a magnificent building with octagonal and bay windows, and apartments with 14-foot hand-carved oak ceilings. It was completed by 1884 and fully rented by opening day.

According to the building bureau, by 1886, 778 buildings were reported going up between 59th and 110th streets. New York's building blitz meant that even those with moderate incomes could become homeowners in the city's outer fringes. Boston was developing its Dorchester and Brookline areas and Chicago touted almost a hundred suburbs connected by rail.

While developers spared no expense to construct dwellings that would attract the well-to-do and upper-middle class, any thought for comfort and beauty was strikingly absent in buildings that housed the poor wage earners. Landlords shamelessly packed in as many families as they could to increase their income. New York's situation was the worst. Dumbbell tenements (named because of their pattern) located in the Lower East Side were seven or eight stories high. Only one room in each apartment received any sunlight or air, and toilet and bathing facilities were inadequate. To save rent, it wasn't unusual for two or three families to share a three- or four-room flat.

Masses of these buildings, over 30,000 by the late 1880s, sprawled in pockets all over New York City. This type of housing blight wasn't unique to New York. South Boston offered its poor three-story wooden firetraps. For low-wage earners in Chicago, Cincinnati, and St. Louis, run-down, single-family shanties were available. In Detroit,

William "Boss" Tweed. Tweed came from a Scottish immigrant family and was the youngest of six children. He grew up on Cherry Street, a middle-class neighborhood in Manhattan. He followed in his father's footsteps for a while as a chair-maker. He was successful but felt that his work lacked excitement. He started a volunteer fire company, and then discovered that the way to the good life was through politics. In 1852 he was elected a Democratic alderman in New York City. He was elected to Congress in 1853, and in 1856 he became chairman of the New York City Board of Commissioners. In 1868, he became the Grand Sachem of Tammany Hall, giving him almost complete control of the Democratic party. From this position, he was able to control votes, accept bribes, and involve himself in a whole series of schemes to overbill the city for various services. He and his associates came to epitomize urban political corruption.

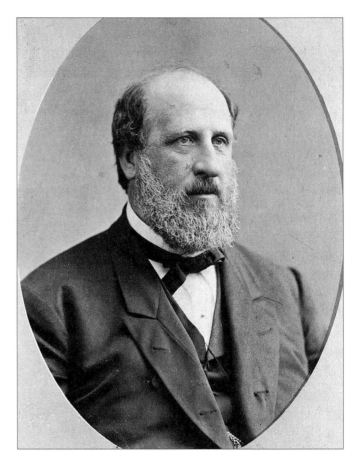

Milwaukee, Omaha, and Seattle, immigrants lived in warehouses and single-family homes that had been converted for multiple occupancy.

For blacks, the situation was worse. Soon after the Civil War, southern states had adopted Black Codes that kept the freed slaves in a stranglehold. They might be free, but they had to work for whites at such low pay or under such unfair conditions that they could never advance. Blacks who escaped to southern cities like Charleston, South Carolina, New Orleans, and Richmond were forced to live in old slave quarters, buildings that had few windows, poor ventilation, and dirt floors.

There was a bit of hope during the Reconstruction years; some blacks were able to improve their situation and a black middle class emerged, establishing small businesses, entering the professions, and obtaining property. Some even founded banks and insurance companies. Maggie Lena Walker became the first female bank president in the country when she formed the St. Luke Penny Savings Bank in Richmond in 1903. Others became doctors, lawyers, nurses, or teachers. A 1900 census showed that 158,000 blacks owned their own farms in the South, but for most blacks in rural areas farm tenancy and sharecropping former slaveowners' land was the rule. Blacks rarely had the means to buy land, and even when they had, most white landowners wouldn't sell to them.

A Supreme Court decision in 1896, *Plessy v. Ferguson,* destroyed the aspirations of many blacks for more equal treatment. The decision stated that while states couldn't discriminate, individuals could, and that "separate but equal" public facilities were not discriminatory. One by one, southern states adopted laws that virtually stripped blacks of their voting rights, and many began migrating from the South by 1890. From 1900 to 1910, when discrimination became especially severe in the South, black migration increased to a rate that was seven times as high as whites.

Initially, while blacks lived in the cities' poorer areas, the division wasn't as pronounced as it became later on. In *His Eye Is on the Sparrow,* Ethel Waters, a successful black actress and performer, talks about living on Clifton Street in "The Bloody Eighth," Philadelphia's

Tweed's greed reached outrageous proportions. A courthouse in City Hall Park that should have cost $250,000 escalated to $13 million, and was still not finished after eight years. Tweed took credit for the city's prosperity and few people criticized him at first. He was, in fact, paying off reporters, but this tactic did not work with two journals, *Harper's Weekly* and its sister publication *Harper's Monthly*. Thomas Nast, the German-born artist and cartoonist who worked for *Harper's*, consistently portrayed Tweed as a corrupt, gloating buffoon.

prostitution district. Prostitution was legal at the time, and Waters, who lived in a three-room shanty off an alley, describes a relatively peaceful coexistence in 1905. "The Bloody Eighth at that time was not exclusively a Negro slum. We had plenty of white neighbors,

Hunkies [people of East European origin] and Jews, and some Chinese. The few respectable families, white and black, forced by circumstances to live in that slum kept to themselves as much as possible. I didn't know much about color then. There was no racial prejudice at all in that big melting pot running over with vice and crime, violence, poverty and corruption."

By 1910, more than a million blacks populated major cities. Washington, D.C., had the largest black population of any city at that time. In the *Journal of Negro History,* a collection of letters written from 1916 to 1918 by blacks who had migrated north, the overall mood is hopeful. But that optimism would change. In 1910, blacks lived within white neighborhoods in Chicago, with concentrations ranging between 22 percent and 61 percent. Ten years later, racial divisions would become much more marked when concentrations jumped to between 77 percent and 87 percent. As more blacks came into areas that had been traditionally mixed, whites fled. Slums arose that housed primarily ill-educated southern migrants. Meanwhile, older, established blacks who had achieved success as clergymen, educators, small businessmen, public officials, and doctors tried to move out of these neighborhoods, but couldn't because of bias. Thus was born the black ghetto.

The contrast between rich and poor had become more pronounced by the turn of the century, and by 1892 there were over 4,000 millionaires in the country. For much of the 19th century, money for business investment was drawn mostly from a firm's savings. But some firms were beginning to accumulate a much larger amount of investment funds. As a result, commercial and savings banks, life insurance companies, and investment houses appeared, serving as middlemen between investors and business firms who needed the

"Who stole the people's money," asks Thomas Nast in his most famous cartoon about "Boss" Tweed's "ring." Tweed and his compatriots can only shift blame to each other. Tweed's main partner in corruption was Peter Sweeny, a lawyer and former lobbyist who was savvy at making political deals. Richard Connolly was Tweed's financial expert. Judges, police commissioners, and elected officials were also part of the ring.

capital to grow. By 1900, the stock market had become the key method for amassing enormous funds for new industries.

Rich businessmen built up huge company empires by consolidating many firms into holding companies. This maneuver was also an effective way to eliminate competition. The American Tobacco Company consolidated 162 firms, and U.S. Steel absorbed 200 manufacturing plants and transportation companies. The tycoons who pulled the strings were so successful that by the end of the 19th century 33 percent of the country's manufacturing was controlled by a very powerful 1 percent of America's corporations.

In most cases, this accumulation of wealth was achieved by corruption, ruthlessness, or both. Cornelius Vanderbilt, who merged several large railroads in the 1860s, typified the prevailing attitude when he bellowed to cautioning lawyers, "What do I care about the law? Hain't I got the power?" These men, who gave hefty bribes and contributions to politicians in exchange for their support, claimed to applaud free enterprise but tried their best to obliterate it. John D. Rockefeller founded Standard Oil in 1870 by buying up 80

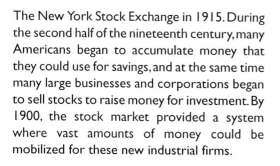

The New York Stock Exchange in 1915. During the second half of the nineteenth century, many Americans began to accumulate money that they could use for savings, and at the same time many large businesses and corporations began to sell stocks to raise money for investment. By 1900, the stock market provided a system where vast amounts of money could be mobilized for these new industrial firms.

percent of the refineries in Cleveland as well as other refineries in four major cities. He created a major monopoly by building barrel factories, warehouses, pipelines, and fleets of freight cars.

There's no question that these industry giants stimulated economic growth. Andrew Carnegie, who made his fortune in American steel mills, once said that American millionaires were the "bees" that made the most money. But Carnegie may have had second thoughts about the tactics millionaires used to acquire their fortunes; he turned away from industrial life in 1901 and became one of America's greatest philanthropists.

Editors, Journalists, and Architects

MANY AMERICANS HAD A LOT TO BE PROUD OF BY THE END of the 19th century—immigrating to a new land, forming a democratic government, and creating a technologically advanced society were significant achievements—but some of the threads woven into the fabric of American life were positively shameful. The systematic destruction of Native Americans and their way of life, the enslavement of and subsequent discrimination against blacks, nativist intolerance of immigrants, the exploitation of workers, and the creation of a wealthy elite who felt they were beyond the law were all part of the American experience.

Many citizens knew about these conditions but didn't acknowledge their existence until a group of journalists, through unflinching reportage, brought them to light. The facts, obtained from the records of congressional and state investigations, court testimony, and city budgets and contracts, jolted America's conscience.

The momentum began in 1890 with the publication of Jacob Riis's *How the Other Half Lives.* Riis, a Danish immigrant who worked as a

Brooklyn Bridge under construction. Brooklyn was the third largest American city by 1860. Its seaport had eight miles of piers, dry docks, grain elevators, and warehouses. Brooklyn residents were proud of their individuality, but their separation from Manhattan by the East River, which was often impassable in the winter, prompted the building of the bridge. Designed by John A. Roebling, it had the longest span of any bridge previously built and it was the first to use suspension cables. Roebling died before completion of the bridge, which was finished by his son, Washington Roebling, who himself became an invalid, suffering the bends from too many trips down into the pressurized caissons used to build the towers. After 13 years of troubled construction, the bridge finally opened on May 24, 1883.

Coney Island, New York, in 1900. After the completion of the Brooklyn Bridge, Coney Island was developed as an elaborate seaside resort in southern Brooklyn. By 1900, factory hours had declined from an average of 70 hours a week to under 60 hours, and the working class needed new leisure activities.

reporter for the *New York Tribune* and the *New York Sun* for 12 years, wrote a gritty portrayal of life in the slums, complete with photos. "We used to go in the small hours of the morning into the worst tenements," he wrote, "to count noses and see if the law against overcrowding was violated, and the sights I saw there gripped my heart until I felt that I must tell of them, or burst. . . ." Riis pioneered the field of exposé journalism. It became a movement in 1902 that was later termed muckraking by President Theodore Roosevelt.

McClure's, launched by Sam S. McClure in 1893, was a monthly magazine that became the first journal to assign in-depth investigatory stories and, eventually, the most influential magazine of its time. McClure had an incredibly hard life. Born in Ireland, McClure came to America at the age of nine with his family after his father died. The McClures settled in Valparaiso, Indiana, and when McClure was 14 he set out on his own, going to work in a nearby town performing chores for a family in exchange for room and board. The boy wore the same threadbare clothes and went to high school without an overcoat during the winter. It took him eight years, sometimes eating only grapes, bread, and soda crackers, to work and pay for his courses at Knox College in Galesburg, Illinois.

Colonel Albert Pope, head of the successful Pope Manufacturing Company, which made bicycles, gave McClure his first real job. Within a few months he became editor of Pope's bicycling magazine, the *Wheelman.* McClure had found his niche. He was good at figuring out what articles his audience wanted and the *Wheelman* became his springboard to a career in journalism.

McClure would later say about his editorial strategy, "I decided to pay my writers for their study rather than for the amount of copy they turned out—put the writer on such a salary as would relieve him of all financial worry and let him master a subject to such a degree that he could write on it, if not with the authority of a specialist, at least with such accuracy as could inform the public and meet with the corroboration of experts."

One of McClure's star journalists was Ida Tarbell, an accomplished woman who excelled in editing and writing. Tarbell was already well known for her biographies; her series on Abraham Lincoln made McClure's circulation soar. But it was her 19-part series, *The History of*

48

(continued on page 53)

Fifth Avenue and 51st Street in New York City in 1913. The streets are paved and automobiles have replaced the horse-drawn carriages. It is fashionable to dress conservatively in dark clothing, except for ladies' hats.

Market and Kearney
Streets, showing
Palace Hotel,
San Francisco, Cal.

The intersection of Market and Kearney streets in downtown San Francisco in 1912. The city appears to be totally reconstructed after the 1906 earthquake. Trolleys and high-rise buildings with elevators were not possible before the development of electric generators and transmission lines.

RETAIL BUSINESS CENTER OF MARKET STREET BY NIGHT,
SAN FRANCISCO, CAL.

Market Street, the downtown business center of San Francisco, at night in 1912. The warm glow of electric lighting changed the appearance of cities and made nightlife more inviting.

Tremont Street near the Mall in Boston in 1916. Open areas and public parks invited people to come out and enjoy the diverse street life of the cities.

(continued from page 48)

the Standard Oil Company, which began in November 1902, that made her famous. John D. Rockefeller's Standard Oil Company was the most important trust at the time and Tarbell had meticulously worked on the series for about a year, documenting the illegal manipulations of Rockefeller's massive monopoly.

When she wrote about railroad freight clerks tipping off Standard Oil officials about shipments from independent oil producers and the subsequent sidetracking of those shipments en route, a company executive demanded of Tarbell, "Where did you get that stuff?" Tarbell was good, and her thoroughness prompted McClure to reward her with stock in his magazine as a bonus.

One of Tarbell's colleagues was Lincoln Steffens. Steffens's series *The Shame of the Cities* began with an article entitled "Tweed Days in St. Louis," a description of St. Louis's widespread corruption. His disclosures included findings from a grand jury investigation; during a 10-year period, virtually every ordinance and franchise granted in St. Louis had been finalized because the legislators were paid money. Steffens wrote about other cities affected by graft and bribes—Minneapolis, Pittsburgh, and Philadelphia, as well as the partial reform taking place in Chicago and New York.

After witnessing the success of *McClure's,* other magazines like *Cosmopolitan* and *Collier's* jumped on the bandwagon. So did fiction writers. Stephen Crane, who penned *Maggie: A Girl of the Streets*, and Upton Sinclair, author of *The Jungle,* wrote stories based on the grim city conditions that existed. Sinclair's novel about the awful, unsanitary practices of the meat industry was instrumental in making Congress pass a federal meat inspection law in 1906. The muckraking era, which lasted until 1912, was the first time that journalists and writers had relentlessly exposed society's ills.

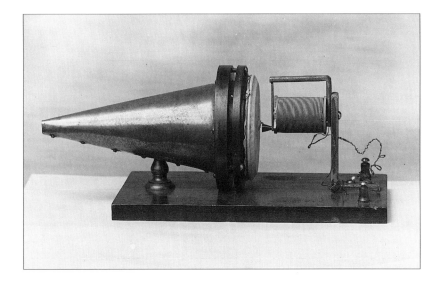

The transmitting and receiving elements of Bell's first telephone.

Cities at this time were beginning to achieve a new look. Large parks were constructed for two reasons. City planners felt that the "softening" effects of parks would provide some relief for the immigrants crowded into tenements, helping them become better citizens. The parks also increased the property values of the surrounding areas, bringing in added rent revenues. Architects Frederick Law Olmsted and Calvert Vaux were chosen to oversee the construction of New York's Central Park.

At over 840 acres, Central Park was the first large-scale park in the country, and Olmsted, named as architect-in-chief in 1857, wanted to create a fragile oasis, a place that offered rural quiet to everyone. His

Thomas Alva Edison. Edison not only invented the light bulb but designed power plants and generators to make the entire system work. Before the electric light bulb, homes were lit by candles, kerosene lanterns, and gaslights. The candlepower of an entire 19th-century village was equivalent to what one modern home receives in illumination today. With electricity, cities experienced major changes. Skyscrapers were erected with electric elevators, and electric engines pulled people and freight.

park had curving roads and paths, long meadows, and sunken roads that concealed traffic. Over 100 different varieties of trees and shrubs were planted to block out the city's presence. The park drives and the use of natural elements, such as the massive rocks along some of the walks constructed as if part of a natural design, were among his innovations. Olmsted established the vocation of landscape architect.

Central Park was considered a masterpiece, and Olmsted would go on to design a total of 17 large parks, including Atlanta's Piedmont Park, a 185-acre site with a greenhouse and conservatory, and Louisville, Kentucky's Cherokee Park, more than 400 acres touted as "a place for artists to paint and for poets to sing about." George Kessler, who worked for Olmsted as a gardener in Central

Edison's West Orange, New Jersey, assembly plant for phonographs. Edison had been simultaneously trying to develop an autographic copying press, a telegraph that would print its messages, and an improved speaker for Bell's telephone. From his work in these areas, he came up with a device that could record and play back music and human voices on wax cylinders.

An advertisement for Edison's new phonographs. Edison headed the National Phonograph Company with a nationwide network of dealers. In 1896 he introduced a spring-motor phonograph, priced at $40, that tripled his previous year's sales. In 1902, he began mass-producing records for his customers.

Edison's incandescent light bulb.

Park, would later utilize Olmsted's influence in his designs for outstanding parks in Kansas City, Cincinnati, Indianapolis, and Dallas.

So too would H. W. S. Cleveland, a landscape architect who became friends with Olmsted and went on to design Minneapolis's famous park system in the 1880s. Cleveland believed that the grid pattern of urban blocks robbed cities of their uniqueness. His plan

The daughter of pioneer settlers, Ida Tarbell became one of the most respected and famous "muckraking" journalists of her day. She attended Allegheny College in the 1870s, the only woman in her class. After working briefly as a teacher and editor, she went to Paris to develop a career as a freelance writer. She met S. S. McClure and began to write for his new, provocative magazine, *McClure's*. Her 19-part series *History of the Standard Oil Company* was a brutally honest portrait of Rockefeller's oil empire and its illegal and monopolistic business dealings. In 1911, nine years after the series first appeared, the Supreme Court ordered the monopoly dissolved.

was to break the grid pattern in Minneapolis with parks and parkways, and he succeeded. Instead of a park here and a park there, he created parks that complemented the natural topography, running along the Mississippi River as well as the area's chain of lakes. He planned his parkways so that the vistas were always

Though best known for his Civil War novel *The Red Badge of Courage*, Stephen Crane was another popular muckraking writer. His book *Maggie: A Girl of the Streets*, published in 1893, shocked readers with its gritty depiction of slum life and poverty.

different and lovely. Artistically speaking, Minneapolis was considered one giant park.

Because of the successful transformation of places such as Minneapolis, by 1890 city planners were beginning to focus more and more on landscaping, architecture, and engineering that was open-ended and unconfined in feel. This trend was called the City Beautiful Movement and it made its debut at the World's Columbian Exposition at Chicago in 1893.

The fair's supervisor, Daniel Burnham, was also a well-known architect and he organized a team of notables in their field—Frederick Law Olmsted and Louis Sullivan were among them. "White City," a beautiful collection of low, dazzling white neoclassical buildings, was constructed in Jackson Park on Chicago's southern lakefront. Burnham and his associates returned to Chicago in 1906 when the Commercial Club of Chicago requested a major city design, later known as the Burnham Plan. The Burnham Plan, which recommended such additions as a new railroad terminal, an east-west boulevard, and the development of lakefront parks and beaches, was accepted by the city council in 1910 and was a key factor in Chicago's development for the next 50 years.

The City Beautiful Movement initiated a crop of new courthouses, libraries, and government centers in other cities. In 1900, Burnham and some of the planners from the Chicago Fair were commissioned to undertake a beautification project for Washington, D.C. The Pennsylvania Railroad was persuaded to remove its tracks from the mall and construct a new central station with the cooperation of the Baltimore & Ohio Railroad. With this improvement, the commission turned the mall into a commanding expanse between the Capitol Building and the Potomac River, adding new monuments and Rock Creek Park.

The unconfined feeling that architects sought in urban spaces was transferred skyward with the availability of high-quality steel for construction. The Bessemer converter, named after its inventor, Sir

Henry Bessemer of England, could not only produce high-quality steel but large quantities of it. Steel mills appeared in the U.S., and by the mid-1870s they were producing 50 percent more steel than British mills. Steel was stronger, more lightweight, and more flexible than

The "Speedway" along the Harlem River in 1900, later to be named Harlem River Drive.

cast iron. It was used by John Roebling in the construction of the world's longest suspension bridge of that time, the Brooklyn Bridge, completed in 1883 after Roebling's death. The Brooklyn Bridge, spanning the East River between Brooklyn and Manhattan, had a

63

steel-cable suspension system and was considered the greatest American engineering feat of its time.

In 1885, Chicago became home to the first modern skyscraper, the 10-story Home Insurance Building, made possible by a complete steel skeleton within the stone. Once the technique of constructing tall buildings with steel skeleton beams was perfected and electric elevators were invented, higher buildings began to appear everywhere. Architect Louis Sullivan, one of the principals in the team responsible for the Chicago World's Fair, was the initiator of some of the skyscraper's trademark features—expansive windows and sheer lines. Sullivan used steel girders in his famous ten-story Wainwright Building in St. Louis, finished in 1891.

While grand and exciting, these efforts to beautify cities were mostly aimed at commercial districts or areas in which government workers lived. The slums and poor districts weren't touched and the disparities became so evident that in 1909 the first conference on city planning was held in Washington, D.C.

Progressives and Reformers

IT WAS THE SIGHT OF POOR PEOPLE FIGHTING FOR decaying vegetables in London that riveted Jane Addams and made her choose her life's work. Born in Cedarville, Illinois, Addams came from a privileged family. Her father had been a successful businessman and former Republican state senator who encouraged his daughter's achievements. Addams attended Rockford Female Seminary and was beginning classes at the Woman's Medical College in Philadelphia when he died. After his death, wrestling with bouts of depression, she dropped her studies. It was during a trip to Europe with her stepmother that Addams witnessed the haunting London scene.

Addams met some of the early social workers who established Toynbee Hall in London, the first settlement house of its kind. To her, the pursuit of art and culture for their own sake had become shallow, and she was attracted to a growing movement of other young people who wanted to help make life better for the poor and destitute. Addams and a friend, Ellen Gates Starr, started Hull House on

Jane Addams. After observing how a settlement house in London could help poor people to help themselves, Addams became determined to establish a similar institution in her native city of Chicago. Hull House, on South Halsted Street near the stockyards, opened in 1889. Eventually, more than 200 social workers lived and worked within a six-block radius of Hull House, serving a community made up of 18 different ethnic groups. Workers put immigrants in touch with organizations such as the Visiting Nurses Association and the Hebrew Relief and Aid Society. There were classes on nutrition, sewing, and dressmaking, and lectures on industrial history. Addams shared a Nobel Peace Prize in 1931 for her work.

Emma Goldman. Unlike Addams, Goldman took a more radical approach to the problems of industrial poverty. She arrived from Russia in 1885 and went to work in the clothing factories of New Haven, Connecticut, where she came into contact with socialists and anarchists. Early in her career, she advocated violence as a means to transform society, but softened her views after 1900—not by very much, however. She lectured on free love and gave out birth control information, and she made a speech in New York City that caused unemployed workers to riot. She opposed the draft and America's involvement in World War I. She was sent to jail many times, and in 1919 she was deported.

Chicago's West Side in 1889 when Addams was 29. Hull House was not the first settlement house in America; the Neighborhood Guild in New York's Lower East Side had that distinction in 1886, but Hull House was to become the basic model for over 400 similar institutions. As Jacob Riis would write, "The Hull House out in Chicago set the pace."

Hull House's original headquarters was an old mansion on South Halsted Street; it eventually expanded to a dozen more buildings that extended over more than a city block. There were 18 different nationalities within the surrounding area, including 10,000 Italians, Germans, Polish and Russian Jews, and many Irish.

Addams understood the immigrants' struggle in adjusting to city life. She wanted to establish a community meeting place to ease their alienation. As a result, she and her helpers hosted different nationalities on different days. Saturday evenings were reserved for Italians; Friday evenings for Germans, and so on. In her book, *Twenty Years at Hull House,* Addams wrote about the reactions of her German guests: "Perhaps the greatest value of the Settlement to them was in placing large and pleasant rooms with musical facilities at their disposal, and in reviving their almost forgotten enthusiasms. I have seen sons and daughters stand in complete surprise as their mother's knitting needles softly beat time to the song she was singing, or her worn face turned rosy under the hand-clapping as she made an old-fashioned courtsey at the end of a German poem."

But the revival of traditions wasn't all that Hull House fostered. Some of the surrounding streets had rear tenements, where the lower floor was used as a stable and an outhouse. Many of the people who lived in the slums were undernourished. They suffered from tuberculosis and many of their babies died. With the help of social work students or interns, Hull House connected with many organizations to help the immigrants improve their lives—the Health Department, the Visiting Nurses Association, and the Hebrew Relief and Aid Society. The settlement house also had five bathrooms available so that the surrounding residents could take baths, a luxury because tubs were not easy to come by. There was a day care center for working mothers and a kitchen with classes in nutrition and food preparation, as well as an art gallery and a music hall.

Hull House spawned some remarkable women. Addams would go on to fight for world peace and shared the Nobel Peace Prize in 1931. Julia Lathrop spearheaded a campaign that established the first juvenile court in the country in Chicago in 1899, and she was instrumental in getting a state child-labor law passed in 1903. Lathrop became the first woman member of the Illinois State Board of Health. Florence Kelley focused on child labor and investigated the sweat shops in the Chicago garment district. She would eventually convince President Theodore Roosevelt to sponsor a national children's conference at the White House.

Seventy-four settlement houses existed nationally by 1897. The women and men who were to become the first social workers came mostly from English or Scotch-Irish families that were fairly prosperous. Most of them were young, grew up in the city, and were well educated; 80 percent had earned their bachelor's degree and 50 percent had done graduate work. They lived at the settlements. While gathering statistics as ammunition for the reforms they wanted to push, the social workers saw firsthand what the poor were experiencing. They viewed their work as a partnership with the neighborhood people in order to help better their lives and stamp out poverty. To accomplish this they lobbied for kindergartens, vocational

68

(continued on page 73)

The elevated railroad that ran along Washburn Avenue in downtown Chicago. The first such elevated commuter trains were powered by steam engines, but electric power soon replaced steam.

Sheridan Drive in Chicago at the turn of the century. Middle- and upper-class urban neighborhoods featured large homes and tree-lined avenues.

The intersection of State and Monroe streets in Chicago around 1910. The concentration of stores and commercial services in downtown areas kept the streets crowded and bustling with shoppers.

Summer Street in Boston in 1916. The architecture of the period often tried to imitate the classical forms of Greek and Roman buildings with their columns and arches, but these touches were purely aesthetic and were unnecessary with steel and concrete structures.

71

Thomas Circle in Washington, D. C., in 1913. Plazas, circles, landscaped gardens, and open areas alleviated the feeling of urban crowding.

(*continued from page 68*)

training, and school nurses, and they made their settlement houses available for union meetings. They wrote articles and books about life in the slums and made others aware of the conditions that existed.

By 1910 there were over 400 settlement houses, 10 of which were specifically for blacks. Blacks who lived in settlement neighborhoods were usually relegated to segregated facilities. This was based partly on the assumption that every neighborhood should have its own center, but was also motivated by the fear that blacks would keep other groups from coming. A few settlements did offer integrated services. Wendell Phillips Settlement in Chicago, started by Hull House residents, was one. Cambridge Neighborhood House had a 10 percent black enrollment in its classes by 1914. While prejudice did exist among some white settlement workers, there were many who were saddened and outraged by the inequities blacks faced. Several helped with the formation of the National Association for the Advancement of Colored People in 1909.

The clergy began questioning how it could better help the poor and oppressed. As with Jane Addams and other social workers, those who followed the new social gospel were jolted into action by incidents they experienced in the city slums. The sights and conditions on the streets had become too compelling to ignore.

Washington Gladden, with Congregational ministries in North Adams and Springfield, Massachusetts, as well as in Columbus, Ohio, became the father of the social gospel movement. He felt a real compassion for the working man and tried to bring both sides together in labor disputes. His mediation skills led to groundbreaking labor and management conferences that he organized in Columbus and Toledo, Ohio. In an effort to smash the grip of a political ring, Gladden even ran for common council

Jewish women factory workers protest child labor in 1909. At the time, almost two million children under the age of 16 were working in factories and fields. Most worked 10- to 12-hour days on farms, exempt from child labor laws that were largely ineffectual anyway. After 1904, Florence Kelley, a lawyer and former Hull House worker, pushed for change and organized the National Child Labor Committee.

in Columbus and spent two years studying civic matters. He lectured extensively and wrote several books.

There were others. William Jewett Tucker, a Congregational minister, was another social gospel advocate. Tucker was a trailblazing instructor at Andover Theological Seminary who introduced one of the first sociology courses ever offered at a theological school. Tucker studied England's church work and its settlement houses and founded Andover House in 1891. Graham Taylor, a fourth-generation minister of the Dutch Reformed Church, followed a similar path. As a professor at Hartford Theological School, he was one of the first to integrate social ethics studies into a theological school curriculum.

Taylor studied Toynbee Hall and the American settlement houses. Here was a tangible way for the church to implement real change, with ministers living in the same neighborhoods as the poor, witnessing their conditions, and working with the people. At the same time, the church settlement would also serve as a training post for new ministers. Taylor felt very strongly about this; he would not take a position at the Chicago Theological Seminary unless he secured permission to start a settlement house. In 1894, Taylor founded Chicago Commons. In a fiery address to an interdenominational meeting of ministers, reform minister Reverend Charles Parkhurst urged his colleagues to step away from the pulpit and get involved: "We have got to give not our old clothes, not our prayers. Those are cheap. You can kneel down on a carpet and pray where it is warm and comfortable. . . ."

The Episcopal Church, Congregationalists, Presbyterians, and Methodists all started settlement houses. Jewish synagogues and

Life in the slums. The streets were dirty, there were not enough schools or playgrounds for children, and some residents had no water supply other than a water pump in their backyard. Peddlers filled the streets, providing what the community needed.

In 1868, Winslow Homer produced this engraving for *Harper's Weekly* showing New England factory workers going home at the end of the workday. There were some early strikes in New England, but by 1900 only 4 percent of American workers were union members. The American Federation of Labor was organized in 1886 and fought for higher wages, shorter hours, and better working conditions, but in its early years the Federation excluded women, blacks, immigrants, and other minorities from membership, severely weakening itself. In 1903, women formed their own labor organization, the Women's Trade Union.

temples, which had already been working closely with the poor in slum areas, organized four settlements by 1895 and by 1910 had established a total of 24. By 1915, there were 2,500 Catholic settlement houses. Charitable organizations like the Salvation Army, a Protestant evangelical group that began in England and came to Pennsylvania in 1880, also tried to provide for the physical needs of the poor, and, among other things, cared for the babies of poor working mothers.

The reformers staunchly believed in what they were doing and felt that individuals were responsible for society and society was responsible for individuals. "What are you going to do about it? is the question of today," stated Jacob Riis when he wrote *How the Other*

A group of garment workers, including a young girl, in a New York City office around 1900. At the turn of the century, the minimum age for child workers was 12, and the maximum workday was 10 hours, but employers routinely ignored these laws. Children who worked looms were doused with cold water so that they would not nod off. The first federal law regulating child labor came in 1916 with the Keating-Owen Act, which prohibited the shipment of goods produced by underage children across state lines, but the law was invalidated by the Supreme Court in 1918. No additional important legislation on this issue was passed until the New Deal of the 1930s.

Machines changed the nature of daily life as well as the routine of the workplace. People slept and rose and adjusted their meal times to the rhythm of the machines, which did not need to eat or sleep. Time took on a new value, the value of what could be produced while the machines were running, and therefore time had to be conserved and spent wisely, like the money it could generate. The pace of urban life was the pace of the machine.

A young girl tends the looms in a textile factory.

78

Child laborers in a glass factory. Because of the heat and the cramped quarters, such boys usually became physical wrecks after a few years.

Half Lives. The years between 1900 and 1920 became known as the Progressive Era because of the national spotlight on urban problems and the resulting reforms.

The Progressive cause was also supported by a young president who had been working on reform during his political ascent. Theodore Roosevelt had been born to privilege but was instilled with a social conscience. His father, Theodore senior, had been an importer

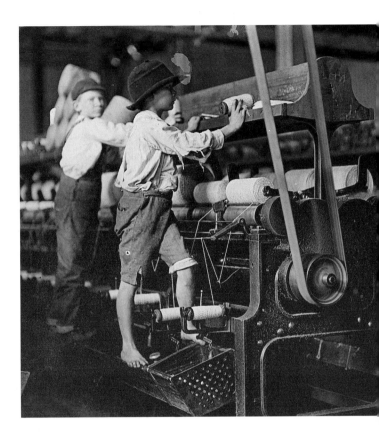

Young boys tend textile machinery. It is not hard to see why industrial accidents were so common.

and a philanthropist who, among other humanitarian moves, had protested at City Hall on behalf of the State Board of Charities against the awful conditions in the city's asylums, where criminals lived alongside the sick and insane. Roosevelt's uncle had been a reformer as well. He had accepted Tammany backing for a Congressional bid in 1870, but he denounced William Tweed and his ballot box tampering a year later and was one of the Committee of Seventy who helped end Tweed's career.

Jacob Riis was a Danish immigrant who came to America in 1870. He worked as a carpenter, a cabinetmaker, and a traveling salesman, among other low-paying jobs. He then decided to become a reporter and write about the conditions of the urban working class. Riis went to work for the *New York Sun,* angering "respectable" people with his stories of slum life and working-class hardship.

As New York's new head of the board of police commissioners in 1895, Roosevelt earnestly began investigating the corruption within his organization by accompanying reporter Jacob Riis on his night rounds on the streets. Elected governor of New York in 1898, he proved to be a thorn in the side of party bosses. He became vice

This photograph of a basement hovel on New York's Lower East Side was taken by Jacob Riis in the late 1880s to illustrate his stories. Flash powder had just been invented, and photographers could now take pictures indoors and in dim light. Tenants of these basements typically paid five cents a night for lodging. Riis's photographs were printed in his book *How the Other Half Lives*, published in 1890. The book became an immediate best-seller.

president in 1900 when William F. McKinley was elected president and took over the presidency in September 1901, when McKinley was assassinated.

Roosevelt saw the federal government as the watchdog of the public good and not beholden to specific interests. He interceded

A vegetable merchant on 135th Street and Lenox Avenue in 1927. By this time, Harlem had grown into a large, thriving community of blacks who had emigrated from the South, and a cultural renaissance was under way.

In Harlem in the 1920s, a group of young boys stage a friendly fight for the camera.

during a long, terrible strike in 1902 called by the United Mine Workers. Realizing that the strike was becoming more and more prolonged, with winter approaching and the need for coal increasing, Roosevelt invited the union workers and the mine owners to the White House for federal arbitration. When the mine owners refused, Roosevelt fought back, threatening to seize the mines by federal troops in order to continue coal production. The owners backed down, and through arbitration the workers won a 10 percent wage increase and a nine-hour workday. It was less than the workers fought for but more than they would have gained without Roosevelt's involvement. And it was the first time in a long while that a president did not side with business.

In his first message to Congress in December 1901, Roosevelt talked about the "abuses connected with the accumulation of great fortunes." He was cautious about lashing out at the wealthy, alluding to the economic benefits that the rich generated for the country, but his concern was voiced. During his presidency, Roosevelt initiated over 40 anti-trust suits. Among his accomplishments were the passage of the Hepburn Railroad Regulation Act, which increased the government's power to regulate railroad rates; passage of the Pure Food and Drug Act, which restricted sale of dangerous and ineffective drugs; and passage of the Meat Inspection Act, spurred by Upton Sinclair's *The Jungle,* a riveting novel about the meat-packing industry. He also won approval for laws that provided compensation to injured workers in the District of Columbia and other areas.

Roosevelt was also the first president to take an aggressive interest in environmental issues. As a young boy, he had spent vacations in the healthy surroundings of the Adirondack Mountains, Long Island, and other outdoor places known for their beauty and clean air. He became a naturalist early on, observing and drawing birds and field animals. During his administration, 250 million acres were added to the national forest system and he helped create the National Forest Service, headed by Gifford Pinchot, the first professionally trained forester.

Expansion and Change

AMERICAN CITIES BEGAN TO EXPAND SIGNIFICANTLY AFTER the 1820s. There were several reasons for this. European cities were becoming overcrowded, and their governments were no longer banning emigration of skilled workers. England was the first to ease its restrictive grip in the 1830s. British immigrants numbered 32,000 in the 1840s and jumped to 247,000 in the 1850s.

Other countries were experiencing famine and government-imposed hardship. Ireland was savaged by a fungus that destroyed the country's potato crop. Its effect was devastating; an acre and a half of potatoes could feed a family of six, and the potato provided the only available food for about one-third of the poor peasants. While blights had attacked Ireland before, the Great Famine, which began in 1845, was compounded by the attitude of the unsympathetic British, who were exporting healthy crops from Ireland to England instead of distributing them to the starving Irish. In their eyes, aiding the poor via public assistance would weaken the people's character. By 1851, about 1.5 million Irish died from hunger and disease.

Transporting new immigrants to America by steamship became a big business, and the major steamship lines set up networks of ticket agencies throughout Europe. Shipping magnate Albert Ballin actually established a village in Hamburg that could accommodate 4,000 people planning to take one of his steamers to America. It had dormitories and dining areas. As most of his immigrant passengers were eastern European Jews, Ballin's Amerika Village had kosher kitchens. It also had a library and daily band concerts.

Between 1846 and 1855, a million and a half Irish immigrated to the United States.

Ireland was not alone in its famine. There were riots in Germany in 1847 because of the shortage of potatoes and bread. In 1848, revolutions broke out in France, Germany, Italy, and Austria-Hungary. In countries like Norway, Sweden, and Switzerland, overpopulation had become a concern. Between 1841 and 1850, a total of more than 1,700,000 people immigrated to the United States.

During this time, Irish immigrants mostly settled in large New England cities. These cities were still in the process of constructing new streets, sewers, waterworks, canals, and railways, and their demand for labor was great. Irish women often found work as servants in middle-class households.

Doctors examining immigrants at the Ellis Island immigration facility. When the ordeal of the overseas journey ended, another began for the immigrants, the bewildering process of getting through Ellis Island. Everything was lines and lanes, and people were closely scrutinized. Until 1911, climbing the stairs to the second-floor examination room was actually an unofficial test—doctors stood in the stairway watching immigrants for any difficulties they might have. The eye examination was the most dreaded. Trachoma was a contagious eye disease that could lead to blindness. Anyone who had it was not allowed to enter the country.

The Ellis Island immigration station in New York Harbor. During the peak of immigration in 1907, between 5,000 and 10,000 immigrants were processed each day. Many had to wait aboard their ship for days until crowding at the station had eased.

Germans, who made up 25 percent of the immigrant population between 1830 and 1880, tended to live in smaller cities like Cincinnati, Buffalo, St. Louis, Dayton, Detroit, and Milwaukee, and worked at skilled trades in the beer industry and as bakers, butchers, cabinetmakers, and tailors. Cincinnati became a prominent Midwest center for German-American Jews and by 1850 there were 3,300. The gold rush lured some to California; Levi Strauss set up a dry goods store in Sacramento and would later become famous for his tough, durable clothing.

Swedish immigrants, looking for religious freedom and land to farm, began settling in the wheat belt of Minnesota and Illinois. But others went toward urban areas; Chicago became the second-largest Swedish city in the world, and its Swedish population sought jobs as laborers, servants, and textile workers.

Between 1820 and 1860, 95 percent of the more than 5 million immigrants who had come to the United States during that time were from northwestern Europe.

Mail-order brides arriving from Europe in 1907. Marriages were performed on Ellis Island until this function was moved to City Hall in Manhattan. Immigration inspectors often served as the witnesses and best men during the ceremonies. Some brides would journey to the Far West to meet their husbands.

Technological innovation was also changing the face of American cities. From 1860 to 1890, 440,000 patents for new inventions were issued. There were almost 500,000 telephones installed in American cities by the 1890s. The typewriter appeared in 1868, the cash register in 1879, and the adding machine in 1891. Thomas Alva Edison's incandescent light bulb encouraged the development of generators and power plants, which provided power for electric lights and other household devices. In 1876, Edison built the first large-scale industrial research laboratory at Menlo Park, New Jersey, later moving it to West Orange.

The creation of steel in the 1850s and its production in large quantities by 1868 fostered new American industries. Pittsburgh's

An arriving immigrant family around 1900. Most immigrants of this period came from small villages and towns. If they could have purchased land in America, many would have become farmers instead of city dwellers. Many did go west, but most wound up in the cities where the factories and work were to be found.

Hester Street on New York's Lower East Side. About 7 out of every 10 eastern European Jews who came through Ellis Island stayed in New York. By 1920, 500,000 Jewish immigrants were crowded into the 1.5-square mile community surrounding Hester Street. Many went to work in the garment industry, which at this time comprised about 16,000 small factories.

strategic location in the iron-ore and coal region of western Pennsylvania and eastern Ohio made it the uncontested steel capital of the country, and other profitable mining regions developed in Minnesota and Birmingham. Railroad companies, which had expanded their lines from 30,000 miles of track in 1860 to 93,000 miles in 1880, relied on the steel industry for their rails and locomotives.

Petroleum became big business when the steel industry needed this product to oil its machines. The first oil well was set up in Titusville, Pennsylvania, in 1859. Other wells were erected in Pennsylvania, Ohio, and in West Virginia. By the 1870s, oil had become the United States's fourth leading export.

It was the ambition of many immigrants to open their own businesses, and some succeeded beyond their wildest dreams. H. J. Heinz made a name for himself in Pittsburgh selling pickles and a kind of tomato paste called "ketchup." Levi Strauss set up a dry goods business in Sacramento, California, and developed tough, durable clothing for miners that evolved into the jeans we wear today. Richard Hellman ran a delicatessen on Columbus Avenue in New York and sold his wife's mayonnaise in a blue-ribboned jar from the deli's countertop.

The new industries and factories were magnets for people looking for work. Factories began locating in cities because of the availability of power and cheap labor. White-collar workers comprised a growing middle class that lived in the cities and had the money to purchase many of the new goods produced by the expanding economy. Low-income workers lived in cities close to their jobs to save money on commuting.

After 1890, the northwest European groups that immigrated here began dropping off because of improved economic opportunities in their native countries and government passage of land reforms. The turmoil and misery plaguing that part of the world shifted southeast.

Land divisions in the Austro-Hungarian Empire restricted peasants to such tiny plots that they couldn't make a living. A French tariff against Italian wines and competition from American fruit markets caused serious, widespread poverty in Italy. And Russian Jews were being persecuted and killed because of their religion.

Large steamship lines like North-German Lloyd, Cunard, and Hamburg-Amerika organized efficient methods of voyaging to the New World and provided better accommodations for their

Liberty in danger from monopoly in this 1881 *Puck* cartoon. The Rockefellers and the Vanderbilts had grown enormously rich and built huge financial and industrial empires, but their activities restricted free enterprise and squeezed many people out of business unfairly.

Children playing in Central Park, New York. In an effort to preserve some part of the city from the frantic construction boom of the late 19th century, New Yorkers convinced the state legislature to save 600 acres for a public park in Manhattan. Frederick Law Olmsted was hired to design Central Park. His finished plan became famous for the many paths that wandered past giant rocks and small stands of trees and created a real sense of nature in the middle of the city. Olmsted went on to design public parks in San Francisco, Brooklyn, Boston, and Chicago.

passengers. It hadn't always been this way; earlier shipping companies were not required to provide food and squeezed passengers into aft steerage sections with little or no ventilation. Many died en route; in 1847, the death toll among poor immigrants was 9 percent.

Ellis Island, a federally regulated immigration station in New York Harbor, officially opened on New Year's Day in 1892. Annie Moore, a 15-year-old girl from County Cork, Ireland, was the first person to come through the station. The port of New York received more immigrants than any other city. If no contagious diseases were found on board their ship, immigrants only needed to pass through customs at Castle Garden, a fort compound built in 1807 at the southern tip of Manhattan. Other immigration stations were established in Philadelphia, Baltimore, and Boston. Galveston, Texas, had an immigration station set up specifically for Jews in response to the vicious pogroms occurring in Russia. About 10,000 Jews were admitted through Galveston between 1907 and 1914.

A Chinese grocery in San Francisco's Chinatown. People with similar ethnic backgrounds often settled in the same urban areas to more easily enjoy shared cultural values, traditional foods, and a familiar language.

By 1907, there were four main European ports from which immigrants left for the United States: Naples, where Italians, Greeks, and Syrians left Europe; Bremen, where Poles, Czechs, Croats, Slovaks, and other Slavs embarked; Liverpool, which accommodated the Irish, British, Swedes, Norwegians, and eastern European Jews; and Hamburg, with mostly eastern European Jews and Scandinavians. Between 1891 and 1900, more than 3.6 million people immigrated to the U.S.; between 1900 and 1910, the figure more than doubled to over 8.7 million.

The older immigrants had already been assimilated into American culture and shared a similarity in looks and religion with the original colonists. The new groups that came in, with their different complexions, religions, and cultures, were resented. The Chinese were specifically singled out in 1882 when the Chinese Exclusion Act was passed; they had been arriving in large numbers in the West and many worked for the western railroads.

The immigrants mostly crowded into the cities where others like them had already paved the way. In the four and a half decades after 1880, 97 percent of Italian immigrants came through New York and most stayed there. Eastern European Jews also tended to stay in New York after coming through Ellis Island; about 7 out of 10 remained. Hungarians tended to settle in Ohio and Cleveland. Most Poles preferred Chicago. By 1900, over two-thirds of those born overseas lived in cities.

FURTHER READING

Bailyn, Bernard, et al. *Great Republic: A History of the American People.* 3rd ed., vol. 2. Lexington, MA: D.C. Heath, 1985.

Bishop, Louis Faugeres. *Myself When Young: Growing Up in New York, 1901–1925.* New York: K. S. Giniger, 1985.

Bridenbaugh, Carl. *Cities in the Wilderness.* New York: Ronald Press, 1938.

Brinkley, Alan, et al. *American History: A Survey.* Vol. 2. New York: McGraw-Hill, 1991.

Bunker, John G. *Harbor and Haven.* Chatsworth, CA: Windsor, 1979.

Chudacoff, Howard P. *The Evolution of American Urban Society.* Englewood Cliffs, NJ: Prentice Hall, 1975.

Daniels, Roger. *Coming to America: A History of Immigration and Ethnicity in American Life.* New York: HarperCollins, 1990.

Groh, George. *The Black Migration: The Journey to Urban America.* New York: Weybright and Talley, 1972.

Hanmer, Trudy. *The Growth of Cities.* New York: Franklin Watts, 1985.

Heckscher, August. *Open Spaces: The Life of American Cities.* New York: Harper and Row, 1977.

Lyon, Peter. *Success Story: The Life and Times of S. S. McClure.* New York: Scribner's Sons, 1963.

McCullough, David. *Mornings on Horseback.* New York: Simon and Schuster, 1981.

McKelvey, Blake. *The Urbanization of America: 1860–1915.* New Jersey: Rutgers University Press, 1963.

Marinbach, Bernard. *Galveston: Ellis Island of the West.* Albany, NY: State University Press, 1983.

Reeves, Pamela. *Ellis Island: Gateway to the American Dream.* New York: Crescent Books, 1991.

Salwen, Peter. *Upper West Side Story.* New York: Abbeville Press, 1989.

Shoenfeld, Oscar, and Helene MacLean. *City Life.* New York: Grossman, 1969.

Smith, Page. *The Rise of Industrial America: A People's History of the Post-Reconstruction Era.* New York: McGraw-Hill, 1984.

Weinberg, Arthur, and Lila Weinberg. *The Muckrakers: 1902–1912.* New York: Simon and Schuster, 1961.

Winther, Oscar. *The Transportation Frontier.* New York: Holt, Rinehart and Winston, 1964.

INDEX

PICTURE CREDITS

LINDA LEUZZI is an author and journalist whose work has been featured in *New York Newsday, Family Circle, Ladies' Home Journal, Weight Watchers, New Woman,* and *The Norton Environmental Reader,* a college textbook. She is a consultant for the Science Museum of Long Island, an interactive science activity center for children and adults in Plandome, New York.